THE
CINEMA

A BRIEF HISTORY
{1821-2025}

BY

WINS DEUS

Special Courtesy

We extend our gratitude to all references and research sources, including Wikipedia, Google, online and printed books, and other scholarly materials. A heartfelt thanks to the contributors who have enriched the world of cinema, including studios, producers, inventors, and filmmakers.

The Cinema - A Brief History: The documentary feature film has been completed in its theatrical version and is set to release this year on OTT platforms and online. It will also be showcased at various film festivals.

JOSEPH NICEP/ORE

NIEPSE

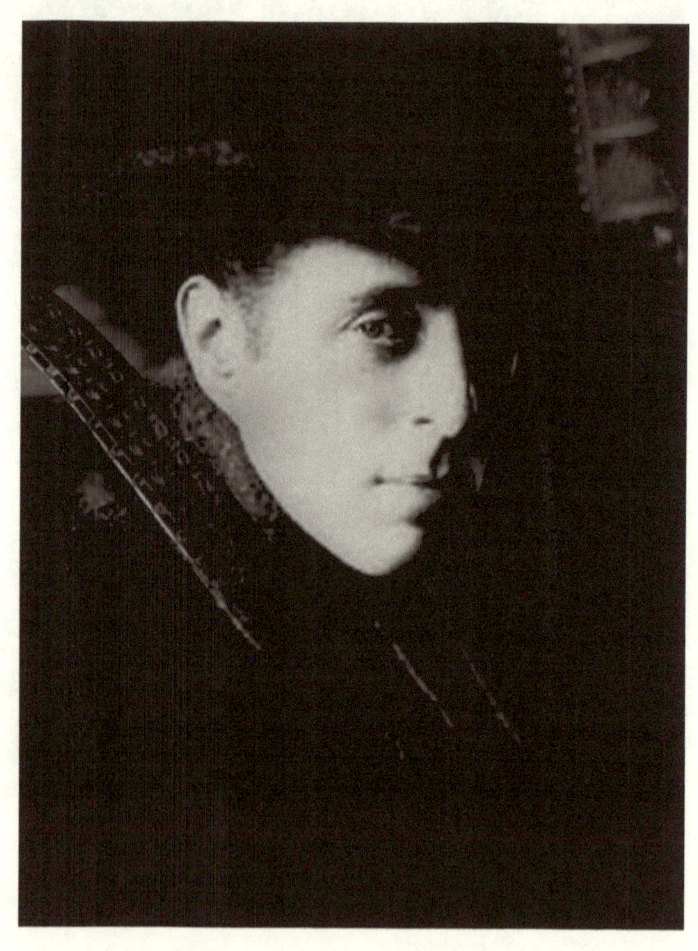

DW GRIFFITH

AL HASSEN

Cinema is the heart, the eyes, the soul of our thoughts and the breath of our lives. It is the human experience captured at length. It is our story. Throughout our culture we as human beings have the ambitious desire to create. And an even stronger desire to capture the essence of our lives for all to see.

Wins Deus

WRITTEN BY

WINS DEUS

ASSOCIATE WRITER

RAEWYN BAILEY

MY VISION

Each and every cinema is a history of human expressions on this planet and our reactions to nature on this planet. It is a catalogue of events, thoughts, concepts and dreams. Cinema is futuristic and because it is as well the past, it captures the present moment, it is created in the moment while involving the future of the past. Imagination is a gift. Life is a blessing. Tragedy is mystic. Love is immortal and forever blending into many different forms. Cinema captures all aspects of the human existence. Some films portrays the best parts of our lives while others validate the darker side of our existence.

The true gift of a filmmaker is to balance all of these throughout their film. For some film making is one-dimensional but for the greats it is multi dimensional. Happiness is developed by thoughts and laughter through the execution of these thoughts. Filmmakers reveal the joy and since joy is transcendental it will be interpreted in many forms, past, present and future as well as happiness, sadness, love and every other human emotion that makes up our stories.

SPECIAL THANKS TO

WILSON CYRIL

SIMON MATHEW

KENRICK AUGUSTA

DR.DIXIT

MANJEET K BENZAL

DEEPAK JAIN

RAEWYN BAILEY

GIJO VIJAYAN

REKHA.S

WILLI KAMARAD

PATRECIO SWANEK

PUNEET R KHARE

EDWARD MUY EBRIDGE

THE CINEMA

A BRIEF HISTORY

The motion picture camera is the ultimate medium for cultural arts and sciences. Through this medium of exposure, we have been united in a modern way by the invention of the motion picture camera since the late 1890's.

In the beginning of the 20th century, motion picture was exhibited as a carnival novelty. This novelty was later developed into the most important tool of communication and entertainment. This became the most popular medium of entertainment for the 20th and 21st Century and steadily became one of the more favoured forms of artistic expression.

The first technological precursor to film was the pinhole camera. Followed by the more advanced camera obscura, which was first described in detail by Alhazen in his Book of Optics in 1021 A.D. and later perfected by Giambattista Della Porta.

Joseph Nicephore Niepce is credited with producing the world's first permanently captured "image", which he called a Heliograph or sun drawing. Niepce's photograph was made in 1826 and was taken from a window looking out across the rooftops of Niepce's home. He used a pewter plate that was sensitised with bitumen Judea. The photograph was made in a camera obscura and took an eight-hour exposure. The photograph resides at the Harry Ranson Humanities Research Center at the University of Texas at Huston. The "image" was discovered by chance in the 1950s, in London, when found along with letters written by Niepce.

In the 1830s this form of picture making was further developed into moving images which were produced on revolving drums and disks. We also saw the invention of the Stroboscope by Simon von Stampfer of Austria, the Phenakistoscope by Joseph Plateau of Belgium and the Zoetrope by William Horner of Great Britain.

To view that which is in motion with one 's own eye is to be present, to be a part of the scene, but to view that which is in motion without ever being present is to experience film in action.

Life moves on without us. Life stands still only when we capture it. Our memories capture our still lives and they are forever embedded in our memory. Some events are more personal histories or more accessible or more memorable than others. Just like our brains the camera can capture all of our experiences and channel our consciousness to a new level of reflection through the looking glass.

On June 19, 1872, under the sponsorship of Leland Stanford, Eadweard Muybridge successfully photographed a horse named "Sallie Gardner". She was captured in fast motion using a series of 24 stereoscopic cameras. The experiment took place on June 11th at the Palo Alto Farm in California with the press present and enthusiastic.

This was the first moment in time for true motion picture. Never before had anyone captured on film a subject in motion. Palo Alto California was the historical place to capture this event.

The exercise was meant to determine whether a running horse ever had all four legs lifted off the ground at once.

The cameras were arranged along a track parallel to the horses, and each camera shutter was controlled by a trip wire which was triggered by the horse's hooves.

The image produced was hauntingly beautiful and successfully documented the first image of beauty and grace in motion.

The spirit of us all is captured in our movement, speech and energy. The spirit of film was first captured by Étienne -Jules Marey in 1882 with his invention of the chronophotographic gun. The chronographic gun recorded all the frames on the same picture and was used for studying animals and human locomotion. A stronger desire to learn more about the relationship between one human being to another, charted the future in storytelling in film.

The Roundhay Garden Scene captured in 1888, was the first known celluloid film recorded.

The second experimental film, Roundhay Garden Scene, was filmed by Louis Le Prince on October 14, 1888, is now known as the earliest surviving motion picture.

On June 21st 1889, William Friese-Greene was issued patent no. 10131 for his 'chronophotographic' camera. The camera captured an image that was sent to Thomas Alva Edison's Laboratory. During this time Thomas Alva Edison was developing a motion picture camera known as the Kinetographe.

Together the two inventors combined their engineering capabilities and created the Cinématographe. Later under the instruction of Thomas Alva Edison, W. K. L. Dickson designed the Kinetiscope in 1893.

As a result of the work of Étienne-Jules Marey and Eadweard Muybridge, many researchers in the late 19th century realized that films were a practical possibility, but the first to design a fully successful apparatus was W. K. L. Dickson. His fully developed camera, called the Kinetograph, was patented in 1891 and took a series of instantaneous photographs on standard Eastman Kodak photographic emulsion, which was coated on to a transparent celluloid strip 35 mm wide.

From paper, to canvas, to celluloid images, great power and human sincerity are captured within these mediums. Film was the first to copy the likeness of an image exactly and transfer its true expression in its entirety and manifest the subject's intentions through movement. If our minds can capture this progression so can our inventions.

The results of W. K. L. Dickson's work were first shown in 1893, using a viewing apparatus, called the Kinetoscope, designed by Dickson. It was contained within a large box, and permitted viewing by only one person at a time by looking through a peephole which required a coin to be inserted after starting the machine. It was not a commercial success in this form, but it paved the way for Charles Francis Jenkins.

Charles Francis Jenkins' projector, the Phantoscope, had its first showing before an audience on June 1894. Louis and Auguste Lumière perfected the Cinématographe, an apparatus that took, printed, and projected film. They gave their first show of projected pictures to an audience in Paris on December 1895.

To see your whole life in front of you is to see great truth. As Aldous Huxley once said, "Experience is not what happens to a man; it is what a man does with what happens to him".

The Edison Company developed its own form of projection, as did various other inventors. Some of these used different film widths and projection speeds, but after a few years the 35-mm wide Edison film and the 16-frames-per-second projection speed of the Lumière Cinématographe became standard. Their American competitor was the American Mutoscope & Biograph Company, which used a new camera designed by Dickson after he left the Edison Company.

Our bodies express much truth and it could be hard to conceal our motivations from others with the language of our bodies but the one gift that we have as human beings on this earth, that is far reaching and unlike any other mammals is the language of speech. Without this obvious and deliberate form of educating our audience of our intentions we are left with only our bodies, movements, and expression to tell a tale. This is where mystery of our true intentions lie.

Australia was known for making the first feature film. In 1906 Charles Tait of Melbourne produced and directed the story of the Kelly Gang, a silent film that ran continuously for 80 minutes. It wasn't until 1911 that other countries started to make full-length feature films. By this time Australia had made 16 full-length feature films. Film production commenced in 1906 in Australia with the production of The Kelly Gang, the first full-length feature film ever made.

Nestor Studio, Hollywood's first movie studio opened in 1912. The film patent wars of the early 20th century led to the spread of film companies across the U.S. Many companies were working with the equipment to which they did not own the rights, thus it could be dangerous to filming in New York. Because of this many film companies packed up and moved setting their sights on the sunny streets of Los Angeles where the weather is always perfect for filming.

Hollywood was an infant during these stages. Everything was new and wonderful. All that Hollywood had during this time was a strong desire and a fresh palette. D.W. Griffith took his acting troop to a vacant lot near Georgia Street in downtown Los Angeles. While there the company decided to explore new territories, traveling several miles north to

Hollywood.   At that time Hollywood was a little village and enjoyed the movie company filming their movie there.

D. W. Griffith was the first to make a motion picture in Hollywood. His 17-minute short film, In Old California, which was released on March 10, 1910, was filmed entirely in the village of Hollywood for the Biograph Company.

The first studio in Hollywood was established by New Jersey based Centaur Co., which wanted to make westerns in California. Hollywood was making its transition from Sleepy Suburb to film capital of the world. By 1920, Hollywood was world famous for being the capital of the United States film industry. Films made before this were a part of what was referred to as the silent era of film. To enhance the viewers experience, silent films were usually accompanied by live musicians and sometimes special effects and even commentary spoken by the showman or projectionist. In Japanese cinema human commentary was common and accepted throughout the silent era and the technical problems were resolved by 1923.

The Birth of a Nation, originally called The Clansman, is a 1915 silent drama film directed by D. W. Griffith. The film was based on the novel and play, The Clansman, both by Thomas Dixon Jr. Griffith co-wrote the screenplay with Frank E. Woods, and co-produced the film with Harry Aitken.

The film chronicles, the relationship of two families during the Civil War, the pro-Union Northern Stonemans and the pro-Confederacy Southern Camerons over the course of several years.

The film, Birth of a Nation, was a big commercial success, but was highly controversial. Its portrayal of African American men (played by white actors in blackface) as unintelligent and sexually aggressive towards white women, and its portrayal of the Ku Klux Klan as a heroic figure attracted much controversy and stirred up great re vote. The Birth of a Nation was banned in several cities. The outcry of racism was so great that Griffith was inspired to produce Intolerance the following year.

A good thing is never as good as it was one of your first experience. And a simple thing is never as great as when it is realized as something great!   Patents make simple processes in film harder for the average novice to mimic.   Patents in film make a motivated filmmaker into a serious filmmaker through its progressions towards acquisition.

These films from the silent era were, Birth of a Nation (1915) D. W. Griffith from the United States, The Cabinet of Dr. Caligari (1919) by Robert Wiene from Germany, Nosferatu (1922) by F. W. Murnau, Potemkin (1925) by Sergei Eisenstein from Russia, The Gold Rush (1925) by Charlie Chaplin from the United States, Metropolis (1926) by Fritz Lang from Germany, Sunrise (1927) by F.W. Murnau from Germany, The Blue Angel (1929) by Josef Von Sternberg from Germany, City Lights (1931) by Charlie Chaplin from the United States.

After the invention of Pronograph, the speaking cinemas future, film changed for all time. Initially, there were technical difficulties in synchronizing images with sounds. It was clear that Edison originally intended to create a sound film system, which would not gain worldwide recognition until the release of "The Jazz Singer" in 1927.

Together with our voices and the sounds of the earth we can paint a greater picture detailed with more indepth human experience through sound. After the release of "The Jazz Singer" in 1927 by Warner Brothers, synchronized dialogue and singing in films was rapidly popularized.

Because of this new era of film demand, there was also a higher demand on film and camera quality.

The Mitchell Camera Corporation was founded in 1919 by Americans Henry Boger and George Alfred Mitchell as the National Motion Picture Repair Co. Their first camera was known as the Mitchell Standard. Mitchell supplied camera movements for Technicolor's Three-Strip camera as well as 65mm and VistaVision conversions before later making complete 65mm and VistaVision cameras (normal and high speed). Mitchell also made a pin-registered background plate, or process, projector.

In 1923 Eastman Kodak introduced a 16mm film stock, principally as a lower cost alternative to 35mm and several camera makers launched models to take advantage of the new market of amateur movie-makers. 16mm cameras continue to be manufactured today by the likes of Bolex, Arri and Aaton many in the Super 16mm and Ultra 16mm formats. Many cameras came before the leaders of today. However,

 the most popular 35 mm cameras in use today are Arri/Arriflex. Panavision models are used for very high-speed filming.

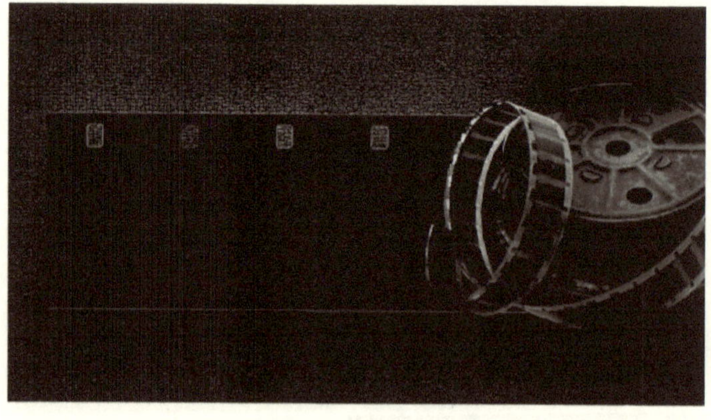

The standardized frame rate for commercial sound film is 24 frames per second. While many other formats exist, the standard commercial width is 35mm. The aspect ratios are 1.66, 1.85 and 2.39 commonly used for anamorphic video. NTSC video (commonly used in North America and Japan) plays at 29.97 frame/s and PAL used in other countries plays at 25 frame/s.

Normally 24 frames is used in the North American area or some European area 25 frames is used. So you have 24 and 60 hertz then you haveb25 and 50 hertz. Now what that means basically as... in the choice we are going to be shooting the sound then you would have to use those particular frames/second and frequencies and ignore to get the same sound. Now you can use that when you have the access for that the frame rates that will you have slow motion or even fast motion basically, we called undertaking or over cranking the camera. Usually that's up...the... set of frame rates.....

Film stock consists of transparent celluloid, acetate or polyester base coated with an emulsion containing light-sensitive chemicals. Cellulose nitrate was the first type of film base used to record motion pictures but due to its flammability was replaced by safer materials. Stock widths and the film format for images on the reel have had a rich history, though most large productions are still film done and distributed to theaters as 35 mm prints. Many of the technical difficulties involving film and video, concern translation, between the formats. Video aspect ratios are 4:3 for full screen and 16:9 for widescreen.

Anamorphic format refers to the cinematography technique of shooting a widescreen picture on standard 35 mm film or upon other visual recording media with a non-widescreen native aspect ratio. It also refers to the projection format in which a distorted image is 'stretched' by an anamorphic projection lens to recreate the original aspect ratio on the viewing screen. The word "anamorphic" and its derivatives stem from the Greek words meaning formed again.

Light hits the eye! Images appear and the highlights of our lives are in three-dimensional form. After this we are inspired to relate to these figures. After that we are inspired to relate to their cause.

The First Feature Film, "The Birth of a Nation", was the new standard for all films to follow with. Through its linear construction and shot arrangement as well as production, coordination and execution, it was the first film of this kind to become a legend for all films to come.

Birth of a Nation was the first film to set the stage for film making as an art. In Birth of a Nation D.W. Griffith utilized crosscutting (parallel editing) effectively particularly at the climax when a number of editing tracks play off of one another. He also portrayed battle scenes with action in one set of shots moving from left to right and while action in another moves from right to left.

The D. W. Griffith film, A Birth of a Nation, was the first film to revolutionize the use of insert shots, close-ups of objects other than faces, which was established early in 1914. These shots were to represent symbolism in a story. They were another way of connecting the story through images. In 1914 "The Avenging Conscience" made extensive use of close ups of hands clutching and feet tapping the ground as a means of emphasizing those parts of the body to portrait psychological attention.

Insert shots detail a story in depth. They can paint a psychological tale that is not fully told by the immediate capture of the forward depth of character representation. In order to process these images correctly with an audience the filmmaker has to understand how the audience perceives. An advanced continuity technique is also a unique advantage in film making. It involves detailing the movement of actors from one location to another neighboring location. At best this type of transition had previously been dealt with by having the direction of the two actors corresponding on the screen.

Unusual angles and complex stage settings are viewed by audience's today, due in part to two German directors' style of film making, in the early 1900's.

In 1919s, "The Cabinet of Dr. Caligari" by Robert Wiene and F.W. Murnau's Nosferatu. These camera angles and complex stage settings are prevalently used. The latter is also credited with perfecting the use of visual language in 1924 in "The Last Laugh", a film about a lonely man who is ridiculed by others.

All this hardly concerned European Cinema, where the few reverse-angle cuts used were mostly between a watcher and what he sees from his point of view, both being filmed from a fairly distant shot.

The contributions from different parts of the world have gathered to make the perfect vision to give audiences a cinematically technical artistic mirror of the world we live in. Through their technique they are manifesting many aspects of human evolution through conceptual imagery. However, at the end of the war some of the brighter young directors such as Lubitsch started using a few reverse-angle cuts, mostly in association with Point of View cutting.

The use of flashback structures continued to develop in this period, and the usual way of entering and leaving a flashback was through a dissolve. These flashbacks allowed audiences to become a part of the story further and through flashback dissolves, the audience could psychologically connect the incident with the subject of importance.

The Vitagraph companies "The Man That Might Have Been" directed by William Humphrey in 1914, is even more complex, with a series of reveries and flash-backs that contrast the protagonist's passage through life. In this film dissolves are used both to enter and leave the flashbacks. Fades are also used for these purposes in this and other films of the same period. Flashback transitions in other films also use irising and even straight cuts.

The general trend in the development of cinema, led from the United States, was towards using the newly developed and specifically filmic devices for the expression of the narrative within film. These were then fused with the standard dramatic structures already in use in commercial theatre to produce truly engaging stories. D. W. Griffith enjoyed the high standing among American directors in the industry, because of the dramatic excitement he conveyed to the audience through his films. But there were others who also considered major figures at the time. The first of these was Cecil B. DeMille, whose films, such as 1915s 'The Cheat', brought out the moral dilemmas facing their characters in a more subtle way than Griffith. Furthermore, DeMille also seems to be in closer touch with the reality of contemporary American life. Maurice Tourneur was also highly ranked both for the pictorial beauty of his films and his subtle handling fantastical frames. At the same time, he was also capable of getting great naturalism from the actors at appropriate moments, as in 1917's A Girl's Folly.

Film industry was burgeoning and on the rise in 1914 in Europe. Filmmakers were establishing their specific styles and creatively film making was beginning to become more than one-dimensional. At such a distinguishing time in movie making the flow of groundbreaking film artistry was brought to a sudden halt by the war.

In Sweden, Victor Sjöström made a series of films that combined the realities of people's lives with their surroundings in a visually striking manner. Meanwhile, Mauritz Stiller was developing sophisticated comedy to an entirely new level.

In Germany, Ernst Lubitsch derived his inspiration from the bourgeois comedy in spectacle of Max Reinhardt's stage work, applying this to his own films, Die Puppe (The Doll), Die Austernprinzessin (The Oyster Princess) and Madame Dubarry.

While World War 1 had staged in Europe, Hollywood was making movies, beginning with the great and innovative works of D. W. Griffith such as The Birth of a Nation (1914) and Intolerance (1916). However in the 1920s, European filmmakers such as Sergei Eisenstein, F. W. Murnau, and Fritz Lang, in many ways inspired by the meteoric war-time film making progress of the Americans

Griffith, Charlie Chaplin, Buster Keaton and many others, quickly caught up with the American film makers and continued to further advance this medium.

Following the end of World War II in the 1940s, the next decade, the 1950s, marked a 'Golden Age' for non-English cinema especially, Asian cinema. Many of the most critically acclaimed Asian directors of all time were making films during this decade including YasujirōOzu's, Satyajit Ray, Kenji Mizoguchi, Raj Kapoor, MikioNaruse and Guru Dutt. Mumbai-centered Bollywood, the Indian film industry's Hindi cinema, Tamil Nādu's Tamil films, from Kerala Malayalam films, Telugu and Bengali films which produces the largest number of films in the world.Latin American Cinema refers to its main centers of production as being Mexico, Argentina, Brazil, and Cuba. Latin American cinema flourished after the introduction of sound, which created a linguistic barrier for the export of Hollywood films.

Shooting in other countries allowed for the films to have a new feeling. The visual look was more authentic and audiences were responding to this method with excitement through their pocket books. Due to the film's new locations and real outdoor scenes, lighting and camera lenses, as well as other technical tools were either invented or modified to suit the needs of this new era in film.

By the late 1960's however, Hollywood filmmakers were beginning to make more innovative and groundbreaking films that reflected the social revolution taken over much of the western world such as Bonnie and Clyde (1967), A Space Odyssey (1968), Midnight Cowboy (1969).

In Japanese cinema, the academy award winning director Akira Kurosawa produced Yojimbo (1961), which like many of his other movies had a profound influence all over the world. The influence of this film is most apparent in Sergio Leone's, A Fistful of Dollars (1964), and Walter Hill's Last Man Standing. Yojimbo is also the origin of "Man with No Name" trend.

The most important films prior to the "New Hollywood" era were many. These films' standards navigated our films into the remarkable visual epics that our storytelling through this medium today.

During the 1930's despite efforts to draw audiences, such as offering concessions, nightly drawings and giveaways, the depression catches up with the studios, and many go into receivership or bankruptcy.

There was a rash of takeovers and mergers. However, this didn't stop the film industry.

The demand for entertainment was still of concern and enhancing a film's quality was still of importance.   In 1934 Three-color Technicolor is briefly in a live action film. Also, in 1934 the Production Code Administration begins enforcing set of rules designed to ensure morality in the movies. Due to this enforcement filmmakers turn to making light romantic screwball comedy.   Then also in 1934 Farns worth produces the first demonstration of a working television system and in 1935 Eastman Kodak develops Kodachrome color film. Becky Sharp is the first all color feature length film.

Later in 1939 Gone with the Wind is released. It relies heavily on special effects such as painted glass mats and optical compositing to create the illusion of spacious plantation mansions and daring rides through burning cities. Additionally, in 1939 the New York World's Fair shows television to the public and exhibits the first public demonstration of 3-D Movies. Later the same year regular television broadcasting begins.

In 1953 "House of Wax" was an early example of the 3-D film craze of the 1950s. The film was the first 3-D color feature released by an American studio, and the first 3-D feature film released by a major studio. "The Stewardess" is released in 3-D and is a huge hit. It used a single strip 3-D process with the left and right frames anamorphically squeezed on to one film. Chis J. Condon designed the 3D acquisition and projection lenses.

3D has been in existence in some form since 1915. The purpose of stereoscopic or 3D cinema is to enhance the perception of depth of the moviegoer. Our 3D is typically shot with cameras that positioned, two cameras either side by side or perpendicular to each other on various types of three camera systems.

This excites the movement of cable and cable reaches its mature form, becoming a means for delivering new and varied types of programming through specialty and pay-per-view channels. In 1977 Lucas' Star Wars and Spielberg's Close Encounters of The Third Kind are released and are hits, relying on good storytelling but also breaking into new special effects territory.

The eighties was a time for more is better, bigger is better, and faster is well, always faster! With this attitude we had to bring our capabilities to an even higher place. So, computers for individual use were developed rapidly in power and speed and infiltrated the film business.

After this in the early 90's came computer based non-linear editing systems and within a few short years they dominated post-production. Likewise, digital media for sound recording became the norm.

Moving into the 90's computer generated special effects were peaking in film. In

Terminator Two they were so visually stunning that it firmly established the computer as the most powerful special effects tool yet developed.

On June 19th 1999 digital cinema demonstration to the public began in four theatres, two on the West coast and two on the East coast. Lucas Films and 20th century Fox debuted "Star Wars: Episode 1 – The Phantom Menace" as the first major motion picture theatrically exhibited as digital cinema using a Pluto digital storage system in the D-5 compression format. Also, in 1999 "The Ideal Husband" is shown at Infocom in digital cinema. This was the last demonstration using the Hughes/JVC ILA projector. Later on, in early 2000 "Mission to Mars", "Dinosaur", and "Fantasia" are released by Disney in the digital cinema format. On June 6th, 20th Century Fox, Qwest, Cisco, Texas Instruments, QuVis, Barco Projection Systems, Eastern

Acoustic Works, and Sigma Design Group demonstrate the world's first digital cinema network distribution and exhibition system. The movie was "Titan AE".

On March 5th 2001, director George Lucas shows the "Star Wars" episode 2 trailer, shot entirely in digital 24 frame progressive high definition. Star Wars episode 2 – Attack of the Clones opens in all 94 digital cinema theaters worldwide. The digitally mastered film shot entirely and digital 24 frame progressive high-definition set to be the first film to sketch the digital film photography.

July 17, 2001 Jurassic Park 3 opens at Los Universal Studio Cinemas on two screens in the digital theatre inter mastering DTIM format. Being used for the first time MPEG-2 + constant quality compression based on the

MPEG–2 compression standard. December 17, 2001 Ocean's Eleven opened in 19 Techni color digital cinemas. The 2000s mark the great transitions for film in the digital era. Because animation is very time-consuming and often very expensive to produce, the majority of animation for TV and movies comes from professional animation studios. However, the field of independent animation has existed at least since the 1950s, with animation being produced by independent studios and sometimes by a single person. Several independent animation producers have gone on to enter the professional animation industry.

These new technologies provided audio and visual that in the past only local cinemas had been able to provide: a large, clear widescreen presentation of a film with a full-range, high-quality multi- speaker sound system. Once again industry analysts predicted the demise of the local cinema. Local cinemas will be changing in the 21st century and moving towards digital screens, a new approach which will allow for easier quicker distribution of films (via satellite or hard disks), a development which may give local theaters a reprieve from their predicted demise.

The film world started out with a pinhole! Projected onto many years past the film world is now configured onto hard drives or a P2 card. These memory aspects create a flawless unity between imagery and story. Prior to all of this we had only raw materials which were precious upon configuration. The images created before digital technology were volatile and vulnerable. This made film making precious and special and every moment captured worthy of being transcribed.

HD film started out in 2K format. 2K depicts the level of resolution that a films picture will have. Standard film is shown in the theatre at 4K. This is the beginning stages of digital cinemas.

The cinema is futuristic and delivers to the audience their own present view of an artistically technical experience that subjectively modifies our own human experiences or our dreams thereof.

Filmmakers and technicians are always curious about how to develop our future through film in a conceptual way. Filmmakers consider the future and they inadvertently become the sages of our past and present. Due to such an affinity to express the imagination of the future, film has become extremely technical and able to carry the image of the future as our mind imagines it. As you see it, I see it and another is dreaming it.

The COVID 19 pandemic caused mass disruption worldwide and the film industry is no exception. With sporting events, theatres and other public venues shut down, people were forced to stay indoors. Streaming services became household necessities during pandemic.

From shorter theatrical windows to simultaneous streaming releases, in 2021 the cinema business was challenged like never before. Rather than wait months for digital and Blu-Ray sales to begin, some production companies decided to release their movies digitally early.

Over the past decade, the media and entertainment industry has undergone a revolution. The demand for streaming media skyrocketed with the proliferation of smart phones and the accessibility to the internet. The Over the Top (OTT) wave gave it further momentum by offering on-demand content, based on individual preferences.

In broadcasting, OTT content is the audio, video, and other media content including feature films in high definition delivered over the Internet, without the involvement of a multiple-system operator (MSO) in the control or distribution of the content. It bypasses the traditional means of distribution of such content via the cable, broadcast, and satellite television platforms, or the companies that traditionally act as a controller of these contents.

Netflix, one of the most popular OTT platforms in the world, started in 1997 to disrupt the market leader of renting DVDs/video tapes. Blockbuster, which rented DVDs/video tapes via stores; Netflix did it by mail. The main reason of Netflix success is their efforts of delivering better customer experience and starting a subscription service.

The growth of the CTV industry is also impressive. In the early days of streaming, most audiences connected their PCs to their TVs. Apple launched Apple TV in 2007. It was designed to feed a big-screen TV with the movies, TV shows, music, pod casts, and photos that were on Mac or PC.

Amazon took a different path to becoming a leader in both OTT & CTV industry by launching different video services, starting with Amazon Unbox in 2006
OTT platforms started in India with BigFlix, launched by Reliance Entertainment in 2008 which is India's first OTT platform. Eventually, OTT started thriving in India in 2013 after the

launch of Zee TV and Sony Liv. Disney Hot star came into the OTT world in 2015.

OTT is the ultimate platform for reaching the targeted audience directly with the content and delivering a premium video experience where providers can get immediate user feedback through direct engagement and interaction.

OTT has gained huge popularity in the US, India, Europe and all over the world in a short period of time as it is accessible to numerous viewing devices from any place in the world, at any time. Netflix, Amazon prime, Sony liv, Disney hotstar, Big flix, Voot Viacom and Zee 5 etc. are some of the famous OTT platforms in the world.

Finally, cinema is back again in theaters. In future, cinema would be released simultaneously in theatres and on digital rental with more expanded technologies with the futuristic vision to the world of enjoyments and also informative to human kind.

The never ending days of future and vision.

Wins deus

WINANGEL PRODUCTIONS & WILLWIN PRODUCTIONS
PRESENTS
WINS DEUS FILM
THE CINEMA
A BRIEF HISTORY
DIRECTION SCRIPT & CINEMATOGRAPHY BY WINS DEUS PRODUCED BY MOONTHINKAL CYRIL WILSON WINS DEUS ALEN MATTERS SIMON MATHEW
EXECUTIVE PRODUCERS KENRICK AUGESTA WILLI KAMAARAD DR.DIXIT PATRICIO SCHWANEK CO-PRODUCERS MANJEET K BANSAL ASHOKAN A
MUSIC BY JUAN PABLO DARMANIN ASSOCIATE WRITER RAEWYN BAILLEY REKHA.S RAJINA G ILLIOT
ASSOCIATE CINEMATOGRAPHERS AJUNE K ANTONY WINSON . DS ART BY REJI KOTTARAKKARA SYAM PRASAD EDITORS DIPIN DIVAKARAN ABIN BAHANAN JOY
WWW.WINANGEL.NET
WILLWIN
PRODUCTIONS
dreamfilms GmbH

ഒരു വടക്കൻ
വീരഗാഥ

THE OFFICIAL COMPLETE SERIES
BONANZA

BEN-HUR
WILLIAM WYLER
CHARLTON HESTON JACK HAWKINS
HAYA HARAREET STEPHEN BOYD
KARL TUNBERG SAM ZIMBALIST

NH STUDIOZ
SHOLAY

STAR WARS
THE FORCE AWAKENS
DECEMBER 18
IN 3D, REAL D 3D AND IMAX 3D

MARTINE CAROL
Madame Du Barry

gothic horror collection

That rarest thing
but the cry of a kind of
prey flower speak to
dead....

A film by
Friedrich Wilhelm Murnau

Nosferatu
a symphony of horror

+ bonus films Vampyr by Carl Th. Dreyer
& Le Vampire by Jean Painlevé

Ernst Lubitsch
Collection
ANNA BOLEYN
DIE AUSTERNPRINZESSIN
DIE BERGKATZE
ICH MÖCHTE KEIN MANN SEIN
SUMURUN
KINO
LUBITSCH IN BERLIN
Oyster
Princess
I Don't Want to Be a Man
TWO CLASSIC COMEDIES DIRECTED BY ERNST LUBITSCH

WARNER BROS. SUPREME TRIUMPH
AL JOLSON
THE JAZZ SINGER
MAY McAVOY
WARNER OLAND
Cantor Rosenblatt
A WARNER BROS. PRODUCTION
KINO
DELUXE RESTORED EDITION
F.W. Murnau's
The Last Laugh
starring Emil Jannings
UFA

IN OLD
CALIFORNIA
A REPUBLIC PICTURE

THE
STORY OF THE
KELLY GANG
(By BIOGRAPH)
Specially taken by
Messrs JOHNSON & GIBSON, Melbourne.
An Entirely
NEW and
EXQUISITE
Pictorial
Representation
of
The
Thrilling
Story
of
The KELLYS

CINÉMATOGRAPHE LUMIÈRE

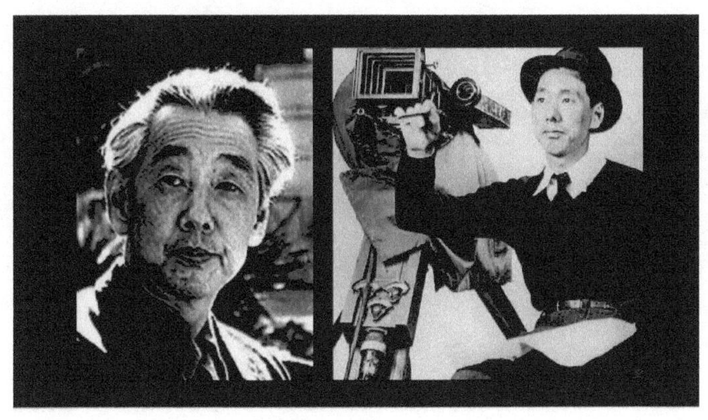

WARNER BROS. SUPREME TRIUMPH
AL JOLSON
IN
"THE JAZZ SINGER"
WITH
MAY McAVOY
WARNER OLAND
Cantor Rosenblatt
DIRECTED BY ALAN CROSLAND
A WARNER BROS. PRODUCTION

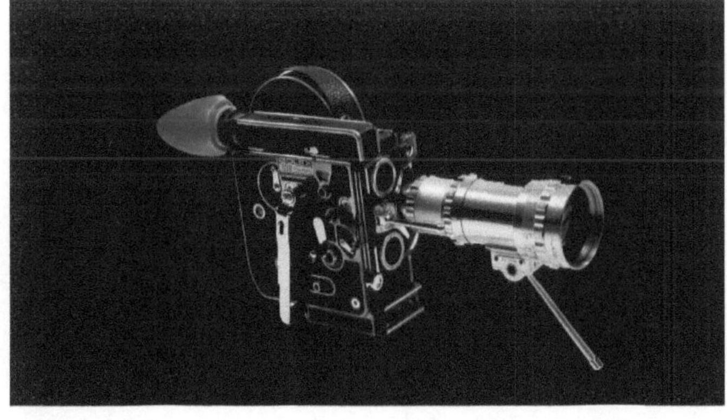

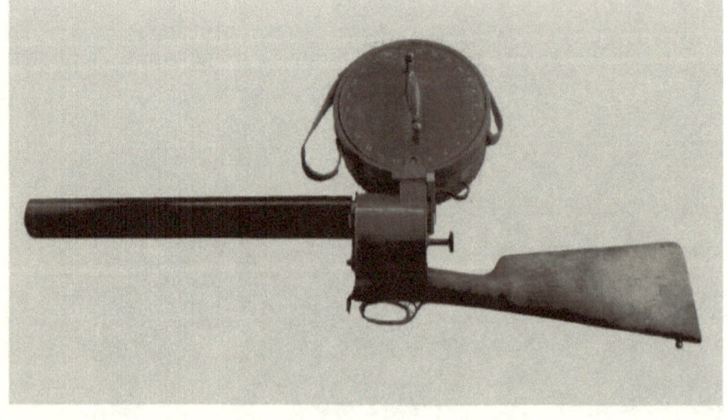

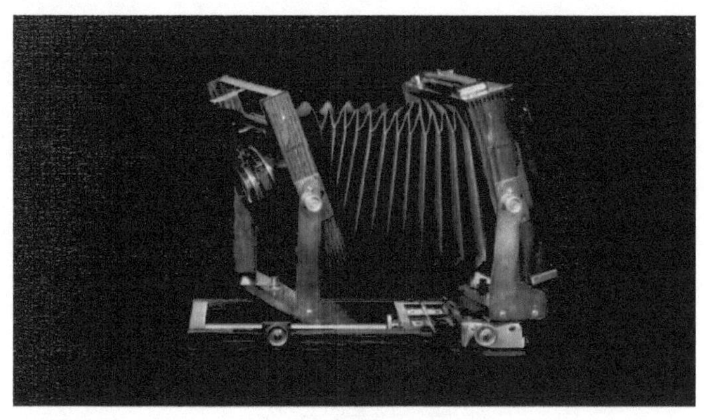

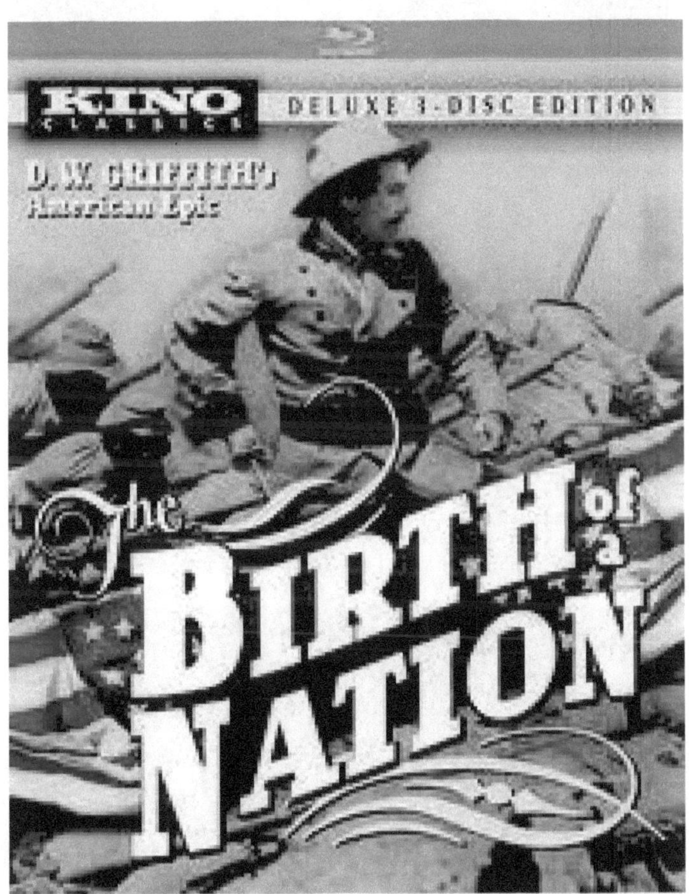

KINO CLASSICS
DELUXE 3-DISC EDITION
D.W. GRIFFITH's
American Epic
The BIRTH of a NATION

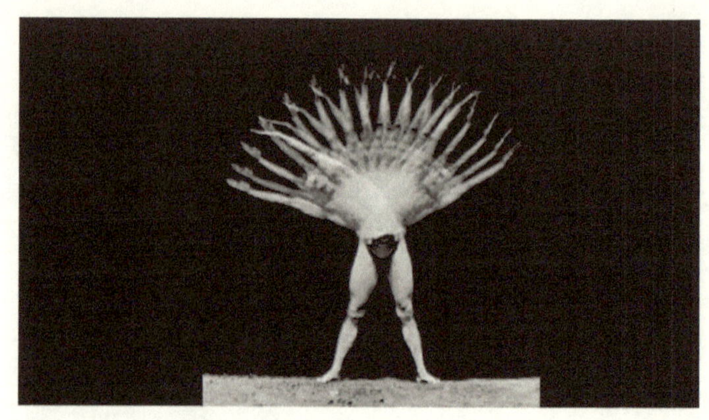

WINANGEL PRODUCTIONS & WILLWIN PRODUCTIONS
PRESENTS
WINS DEUS FILM
THE CINEMA
A BRIEF HISTORY
DIRECTION SCRIPT & CINEMATOGRAPHY BY WINS DEUS PRODUCED BY MOONTHINKAL CYRIL WILSON WINS DEUS ALEN MATTERS SIMON MATHEW
EXECUTIVE PRODUCERS KENRICK AUGESTA WELLI KAMAARAD DR.DIXIT PATRICIO SCHWANEK CO-PRODUCERS MANJEET K BANSAL ASHOKAN A
MUSIC BY JUAN PABLO DARMANIN ASSOCIATE WRITER RAEWYN BAILLEY REKHA.S RAJINA G ILLIOT
ASSOCIATE CINEMATOGRAPHERS AJUNE K ANTONY WINSON DS ART BY REJI KOTTARAKKARA SYAM PRASAD EDITORS DIPIN DIVAKARAN ABIN BAHANAN JOY
WWW.WINANGEL.NET
WILLWIN

dreamfilms

www.ingramcontent.com/pod-product-compliance
Lightning Source LLC
Chambersburg PA
CBHW062229150726
47991CB00006B/2501